PERSONAL GROWTH IS PERSONAL

STUDY GUIDE

Copyright © 2024 by Abram Gomez

Published by Arrows and Stones

All rights reserved. No portion of this book may be reproduced, stored in a retrieval system, or transmitted in any form or by any means—electronic, mechanical, photocopy, recording, scanning, or other—except for brief quotations in critical reviews or articles, without prior written permission of the author.

Scripture quotations marked NLT are taken from the Holy Bible, New Living Translation, copyright © 1996, 2004, 2015 by Tyndale House Foundation. Used by permission of Tyndale House Publishers, Inc., Carol Stream, Illinois 60188. All rights reserved. | Scripture quotations marked MSG are taken from THE MESSAGE, copyright © 1993, 1994, 1995, 1996, 2000, 2001, 2002 by Eugene H. Peterson. Used by permission of NavPress. All rights reserved. Represented by Tyndale House Publishers, Inc. | Scripture quotations marked NIV are taken from the Holy Bible, New International Version®, NIV®. Copyright © 1973, 1978, 1984, 2011 by Biblica, Inc.™ Used by permission of Zondervan. All rights reserved worldwide. www.zondervan.com. The "NIV" and "New International Version" are trademarks registered in the United States Patent and Trademark Office by Biblica, Inc.™ | Scripture quotations marked NKJV are taken from the New King James Version®. Copyright © 1982 by Thomas Nelson. Used by permission. All rights reserved.

For foreign and subsidiary rights, contact the author.

Cover design by Sara Young
Cover photo by: Jeanette G. Zapata Photography

ISBN: 978-1-960678-82-9   1 2 3 4 5 6 7 8 9 10

Printed in the United States of America

SEVEN PERSONAL
WAYS FOR DEVELOPING
YOUR POTENTIAL

PERSONAL GROWTH IS PERSONAL

ABRAM GOMEZ

STUDY GUIDE

ARROWS & STONES

CONTENTS

Chapter 1. Personal Story 6

Chapter 2. Personal Awareness 12

Chapter 3. Personal Mindset 16

Chapter 4. Personal Communication 22

Chapter 5. Personal Environment 28

Chapter 6. Personal Relationships 34

Chapter 7. Personal Habits 40

Chapter 8. Personal Growth 46

Chapter 9. Die Empty 50

Personal Growth Plan 54

7 Bible Verses On Personal Growth 55

Smart Goals Worksheet 56

SWOT Analysis 57

SEVEN PERSONAL WAYS FOR DEVELOPING YOUR POTENTIAL

PERSONAL GROWTH IS PERSONAL

ABRAM GOMEZ

CHAPTER 1

PERSONAL STORY

Growth doesn't just happen, you know. You can grow either by the school of hard knocks, or you can grow by the school of intentionality.

READING TIME

As you read Chapter 1: "Personal Story" in *Personal Growth Is Personal*, reflect on, and respond to the text by answering the following questions.

REFLECT AND TAKE ACTION:

In this chapter, the author states that you have "unused success." What success do you think is waiting for you that has not yet been used?

_____
_____
_____
_____
_____
_____
_____
_____
_____

Do you have a plan for your personal growth, and if so, what is it? If not, use the space below to create a plan, using the author's as general guidance

_____
_____
_____
_____
_____
_____
_____
_____
_____
_____

> *So Samuel grew, and the LORD was with him and let none of his words fall to the ground.*
> —1 Samuel 3:19 (NKJV)

Consider the scripture above and answer the following questions:

What do you think the author of this verse meant by "let none of his words fall to the ground"?

_____
_____
_____
_____
_____
_____
_____

What responsibility did Samuel have to accomplish God's purposes and what responsibility did the Lord have? What does this tell you about the importance of partnering with God to fulfill your potential?

_____
_____
_____
_____
_____
_____
_____
_____

8 | PERSONAL STORY

What in your life do you feel has "fallen to the ground"?

_____
_____
_____
_____
_____
_____
_____
_____

In what areas of your life do you most want to see your growth plan at work? Why?

_____

_____

_____

_____

_____

_____

_____

_____

If you were to fulfill your potential through a growth plan, what is your vision for the impact you would like to have on your environment, relationships, and community?

_____

_____

_____

_____

_____

_____

_____

_____

How do you see your self-awareness at work in your growth toward accomplishing your purpose?

_____
_____
_____
_____
_____
_____
_____
_____
_____

What is your personal story, and why do you think it is valuable to your growth journey and to others?

_____
_____
_____
_____
_____
_____
_____
_____
_____

CHAPTER 2

PERSONAL AWARENESS

We live in a time where we learn a great amount about others, but we don't learn about ourselves.

READING TIME

As you read Chapter 2: "Personal Awareness" in *Personal Growth Is Personal*, reflect on, and respond to the text by answering the following questions.

REFLECT AND TAKE ACTION:

Reflect back to the lowest places in your life. What kind of knowledge, dreams, and ideas were birthed in those places?

_____
_____
_____
_____
_____
_____
_____
_____
_____
_____

Why is surrendering your plans, thoughts, and dreams to God so necessary in order to generate greater self-awareness?

_____
_____
_____
_____
_____
_____
_____
_____
_____
_____

> "O LORD, You have searched me and known me. You know my sitting down and my rising up; You understand my thought afar off. You comprehend my path and my lying down, and are acquainted with all my ways."
>
> —Psalm 139:1-3 (NKJV)

Consider the scripture above and answer the following questions:

Drawing from this Scripture, what has God revealed to you about who He created you to be that you didn't know before?

_____
_____
_____
_____
_____
_____

How does God's intimate knowledge of you impact your desire to know and understand who He created you to be?

_____
_____
_____
_____

The author states that "your misery can become your ministry." What does this mean to you personally? How does it apply to your life?

_____
_____
_____

Do you recognize the gifts that God has deposited within you? What are they?

Think about the closest, most intimate relationship you have. Do you know their story better than your own?

What questions are you wrestling with about where God wants to use your gifts and talents?

CHAPTER 3

PERSONAL MINDSET

It's hard to consistently perform in a manner that is inconsistent with the way you see yourself.

READING TIME

As you read Chapter 3: "Personal Mindset" in *Personal Growth Is Personal*, reflect on, and respond to the text by answering the following questions.

REFLECT AND TAKE ACTION:

What kind of faulty thinking do you find yourself rehearsing (about yourself, work, family, ministry, etc.)?

_____
_____
_____
_____
_____
_____
_____
_____
_____
_____

Think of an opportunity or dream that has been presented to you that you haven't yet moved forward with. What is stopping you?

_____
_____
_____
_____
_____
_____
_____
_____
_____
_____

> *Summing it all up, friends, I'd say you'll do best by filling your minds and meditating on things true, noble, reputable, authentic, compelling, gracious—the best, not the worst; the beautiful, not the ugly; things to praise, not things to curse.*
>
> —Philippians 4:8 (MSG)

Consider the scripture above and answer the following questions:

What do you think it looks like practically to "meditate" over these things that Paul lists in this Scripture?

_____
_____
_____
_____
_____
_____
_____
_____
_____

What are some examples of each item (things that are true, noble, reputable, authentic, compelling, gracious, best, beautiful, and worthy of praise) found in your own life?

_____
_____
_____
_____
_____
_____

If you were to develop a habit of meditating on those things that bring life rather than things that bring death, what kind of impact would this have on your growth?

In what areas of life do you seem to get in your own way the most? What kind of thoughts do you think about those challenges?

_____

_____

_____

_____

_____

_____

_____

_____

How might your thoughts and words be perpetuating those areas where you are stuck? What kind of changes do you want to see?

_____

_____

_____

_____

_____

_____

_____

_____

Refer to the list of things that shape our mindsets (past and current experiences, level of education, circle of friends and family, mentors and leaders, location and culture, and faith). How would you rate the health of these areas in your life right now?

_____
_____
_____
_____
_____
_____
_____
_____

If you could begin to think different thoughts over your greatest insecurities, what would they be?

_____
_____
_____
_____
_____
_____
_____

CHAPTER 4

PERSONAL COMMUNICATION

God has placed within you the authority to have dominion, even over your words.

READING TIME

As you read Chapter 4: "Personal Communication" in *Personal Growth Is Personal*, reflect on, and respond to the text by answering the following questions.

REFLECT AND TAKE ACTION:

Referring back to the reflection questions from Chapter 3, take note of the areas in your life in which your thoughts cause harm. Are your words in agreeance with those thoughts? How so?

_____
_____
_____
_____
_____
_____
_____
_____
_____

How might the words we speak become a kind of self-fulfilling prophecy? How has this shown up in your own life?

_____
_____
_____
_____
_____
_____
_____
_____
_____

> *"For it would have been better for us to serve the Egyptians than that we should die in the wilderness."*
>
> —Exodus 14:12 (NKJV)

Consider the scripture above and answer the following questions:

Why do you think the Israelites made these damaging confessions? What does this say about our tendency to mistake God's goodness and rescue for danger and harm?

_____
_____
_____
_____
_____
_____
_____
_____
_____
_____

How might the Israelites' journey through the wilderness looked differently had their words instead reflected God's grace, mercy, and heart to bless them?

_____
_____
_____
_____
_____

How could you apply this to your own life? What is your "Egypt" and what are you confessing about your Promised Land?

Who in your circle of influence is living the life you want to live? What kinds of words do you hear them speak?

_____
_____
_____
_____
_____
_____
_____
_____
_____

How well are your mind and mouth working together?

_____
_____
_____
_____
_____
_____
_____
_____
_____

What kind of practices do you have in place for improving your communication and cleaning up your speech to align with who you really are as a child of God?

_____
_____
_____
_____
_____
_____
_____
_____

What do you care about and need that you feel you have not adequately vocalized?

_____
_____
_____
_____
_____
_____
_____
_____

CHAPTER 5

PERSONAL ENVIRONMENT

If you desire to grow and change, sometimes, things in your surroundings need to change.

READING TIME

As you read Chapter 5: "Personal Environment" in *Personal Growth Is Personal,* reflect on, and respond to the text by answering the following questions.

REFLECT AND TAKE ACTION:

What kind of environment do you regularly find yourself in? Who are you spending time with? Where do you go? Is it serving you or holding you back?

_____
_____
_____
_____
_____
_____
_____
_____
_____

Think about a time in your life when you were thriving the most. What was your environment like at the time?

_____
_____
_____
_____
_____
_____
_____
_____

> "Now He could do no mighty work there, except that He laid His hands on a few sick people and healed them. And He marveled because of their unbelief."
>
> —Mark 6:5-6 (NKJV)

Consider the scripture above and answer the following questions:

How has unbelief (either your own or someone else's) negatively impacted your progress or work in the past?

_____
_____
_____
_____
_____
_____
_____
_____
_____
_____

What does this Scripture say about the power of believing? What can Jesus do with big faith?

_____
_____
_____
_____
_____
_____
_____

What does belief have to do with the environment we immerse ourselves in?

In what ways, either previously or presently, have you impacted (both negatively and positively) your atmosphere? Describe.

_____
_____
_____
_____
_____
_____
_____
_____
_____

What are some adjustments you can make to your environment that would be more conducive to your mental and spiritual growth?

_____
_____
_____
_____
_____
_____
_____
_____
_____

In this chapter, the author encourages us to "build a firewall of protection around our destiny." What do you think this means, and what does protecting your destiny look like for you?

_____
_____
_____
_____
_____
_____
_____
_____
_____

CHAPTER 6

PERSONAL RELATIONSHIPS

Relationships matter. They are consequential. They affect you—good or bad. They help or hinder you.

READING TIME

As you read Chapter 6: "Personal Relationships" in *Personal Growth Is Personal*, reflect on, and respond to the text by answering the following questions.

REFLECT AND TAKE ACTION:

What role have relationships played in your life? How have they impeded your growth? How have they facilitated it?

_____
_____
_____
_____
_____
_____
_____
_____
_____
_____

How would you rate the quality of your relationships on a scale of 1 (very bad) to 10 (very good)? Explain your choice.

1   2   3   4   5   6   7   8   9   10

_____
_____
_____
_____
_____
_____
_____
_____

> *"Do not be misled: 'Bad company corrupts good character.'"*
> —1 Corinthians 15:33 (NIV)

Consider the scripture above and answer the following questions:

In what ways can the health of our relationships be misleading?

_____
_____
_____
_____
_____
_____
_____
_____
_____
_____

Provide an example of one relationship that corrupted your character or that of someone you know. What kind of counsel would you give yourself if you had to do it over?

_____
_____
_____
_____
_____
_____
_____

Why do you think people are such a powerful influence over our character?

Which relationships have been stumbling blocks to you, and why?

_____
_____
_____
_____
_____
_____
_____

Refer to the 2 Kings 3:11-15 Scripture in this chapter. Can you think of a friendship that changed the course of your future?

_____
_____
_____
_____
_____
_____
_____

Are there any relationships that you need to release? Why or why not?

_____
_____
_____

How could you begin to release those relationships? What's the first step?

Refer to the three types of people the author lists that we all need in our lives. Who is your Barnabas? Paul? Timothy?

CHAPTER 7

PERSONAL HABITS

When what you want to be and what you do are walking together in agreement, you are simply being who you are based on doing what you know.

READING TIME

As you read Chapter 7: "Personal Habits" in *Personal Growth Is Personal*, reflect on, and respond to the text by answering the following questions.

REFLECT AND TAKE ACTION:

What personal habits do you have that serve you well? Which habits are self-defeating?

_____
_____
_____
_____
_____
_____
_____
_____
_____

In what ways do you struggle with developing and maintaining healthy habits? Why do you think this is?

_____
_____
_____
_____
_____
_____
_____
_____
_____
_____

> "Do you not know that those who run in a race all run, but one receives the prize? Run in such a way that you may obtain it. And everyone who competes for the prize is temperate in all things. Now they do it to obtain a perishable crown, but we for an imperishable crown. Therefore I run thus: not with uncertainty. Thus I fight: not as one who beats the air. But I discipline my body and bring it into subjection, lest, when I have preached to others, I myself should become disqualified."
>
> —1 Corinthians 9:24-27 (NKJV)

Consider the scripture above and answer the following questions:

How do you think Paul's depiction of the practice of disciplining our bodies translates to our daily walk toward growth?

_____
_____
_____
_____
_____
_____
_____

What kind of race are you running? Are there any temporal prizes you are after? Eternal prizes?

_____
_____
_____
_____
_____
_____
_____

In what ways does the race that you run impact others and their pursuit of growth?

_____
_____
_____
_____
_____

Which prizes are you competing for that need to take a backseat to imperishable things?

_____
_____
_____
_____
_____
_____

Who do you desire to become?

_____
_____
_____
_____
_____
_____
_____
_____

What beliefs need to change in order for you to become that person?

_____
_____
_____
_____
_____
_____
_____
_____
_____

Refer to Luke 2:46-49 in this chapter. What needs to happen for your desire to find and fulfill your potential to overpower the voices that may discourage you from doing so?

_____
_____
_____
_____
_____
_____
_____
_____

How clear are you on your purpose and do you know the measures you need to put in place in order to accomplish it?

_____
_____
_____
_____
_____
_____
_____
_____

CHAPTER 8

PERSONAL GROWTH

Growth is your friend. Your personal growth is the gift that keeps on giving. Rather than being intimidated by it, lean into it. Dive into it. Meet it head-on.

READING TIME

As you read Chapter 8: "Personal Growth" in Personal Growth Is Personal, *reflect on, and respond to the text by answering the following questions.*

REFLECT AND TAKE ACTION:

Now that you are clearer on your vision of who you want to become, what steps can you take to apply this vision?

_____
_____
_____
_____
_____
_____
_____
_____
_____
_____

Do you ever feel that you "wait" for growth to happen for you? Explain.

_____
_____
_____
_____
_____
_____
_____
_____
_____
_____

> *"So then faith comes by hearing, and hearing by the word of God."*
> —Romans 10:17 (NKJV)

Consider the scripture above and answer the following questions:

How often are you hearing the Word of God? What does your daily time with the Lord look like?

___

Why does a greater measure of faith follow consistent and concerted exposure to God's Word?

___

Refer to the personal growth myths listed in this chapter. Which ones stood out to you? Are there any that resonate with you more deeply than others?

_____
_____
_____
_____
_____
_____

Do you ever feel intimidated by the idea of personal growth? Why or why not? Why do you think it is worth meeting head-on?

_____
_____
_____
_____
_____
_____

If you were to follow a similar growth plan suggested by the author in this chapter, what would it look like for you?

_____
_____
_____
_____
_____
_____

CHAPTER 9

DIE EMPTY

Don't die old; die finished.

READING TIME

As you read Chapter 9: "Die Empty" in *Personal Growth Is Personal*, reflect on, and respond to the text by answering the following questions.

REFLECT AND TAKE ACTION:

What is your impression of what it means to die empty?

_____
_____
_____
_____
_____
_____
_____
_____
_____

What messages (sermons, speeches, counsel from trusted mentors) have profoundly impacted you and changed the way you think and travel through life?

_____
_____
_____
_____
_____
_____
_____
_____
_____
_____

> "Whatever your hand finds to do, do it with your might; for there is no work or device or knowledge or wisdom in the grave where you are going."
>
> —Ecclesiastes 9:10 (NKJV)

Consider the scripture above and answer the following questions:

What does "working with all your might" look like in the places God has planted you right now? How can you honor Him in every work you put your hands to?

_____
_____
_____
_____
_____

How does the inevitability of death inspire you to finish and finish strong, pouring yourself out in everything you do?

_____
_____
_____
_____
_____

What do you think God has called you to do and fulfill while you are alive?

_____
_____
_____
_____
_____

Refer to the list of common reasons that keep people from releasing what's within them (procrastination, neglect, and mindset). Are there any that you identify with more than others?

How can you begin to address these barriers?

Refer to the author's story of the fulfillment of a prophetic word that was spoken over him. What does this tell you about God's intimate involvement in your personal growth journey?

PERSONAL GROWTH PLAN

MY 3 GOALS
- ▸ _____
- ▸ _____
- ▸ _____

BOOKS	
_____	☐
_____	☐
_____	☐
_____	☐
_____	☐
_____	☐
_____	☐

PODCASTS	
_____	☐
_____	☐
_____	☐

CONFERENCES	
_____	☐
_____	☐
_____	☐

NETWORK	
_____	☐
_____	☐
_____	☐

COACHING	
_____	☐
_____	☐
_____	☐

OTHER	
_____	☐
_____	☐
_____	☐

Commit to the Lord what you do, and He will establish your plans.
—Proverbs 16:3

7 BIBLE VERSES ON PERSONAL GROWTH

"Do not neglect the gift that is in you, which was given to you by prophecy with the laying on of the hands of the eldership. Meditate on these things; give yourself entirely to them, that your progress may be evident to all."

—1 Timothy 4:14-15 (NKJV)

"Jesus grew in wisdom and in stature and in favor with God and all the people."

—Luke 2:52 (NLT)

"And the child Samuel grew in stature, and in favor both with the Lord and men."

—1 Samuel 2:26 (NKJV)

"...that you may walk worthy of the Lord, fully pleasing Him, being fruitful in every good work and increasing in the knowledge of God..."

—Colossians 1:10 (NKJV)

"...but grow in the grace and knowledge of our Lord and Savior Jesus Christ. To Him be the glory both now and forever. Amen."

—2 Peter 3:18

"Observe people who are good at their work—skilled workers are always in demand and admired; they don't take a backseat to anyone."

—Proverbs 22:29 (MSG)

"A man's gift makes room for him, and brings him before great men."

—Proverbs 18:16 (NKJV)

SMART GOALS WORKSHEET

S   SPECIFIC *(Describe your goal.)*

M   MEASURABLE *(How can you track progress?)*

 ACHIEVABLE *(Is this possible? How?)*

 RELEVANT *(Does this align with the bigger picture?)*

 TIME *(What is the deadline?)*

SWOT ANALYSIS

S — STRENGTHS

W — WEAKNESSES

O — OPPORTUNITIES

T — THREATS

www.ingramcontent.com/pod-product-compliance
Lightning Source LLC
Chambersburg PA
CBHW062123080426
42734CB00012B/2971